Alexander Tilloch Galt

Canada, 1849 to 1859

Alexander Tilloch Galt

Canada, 1849 to 1859

ISBN/EAN: 9783337185008

Printed in Europe, USA, Canada, Australia, Japan

Cover: Foto ©ninafisch / pixelio.de

More available books at **www.hansebooks.com**

CANADA:

1849 to 1859.

BY

THE HON. A. T. GALT,

FINANCE MINISTER OF CANADA.

QUEBEC:
PRINTED AT THE CANADA GAZETTE OFFICE.

1860.

In issuing another edition of the following sketch of the progress of Canada, during the past decade, advantage has been taken of the opportunity to correct some inaccuracies which had inadvertently been permitted to occur in the first issue.

The object of the writer has only been to give an outline of the features of Canadian progress, without attempting to enlarge upon details. Many subjects of considerable importance have necessarily been passed over, and he can only express his satisfaction that the public has been kind enough to treat the publication with so much indulgence.

Quebec, 1st March, 1860.

CANADA:

1849 TO 1859.

The history and progress of the Colonies of Great Britain must naturally be a subject of deep interest to the people of England, especially since the experiment has been fairly tried of entrusting these dependencies of the empire with local self-government.

On the one hand, it was contended that constitutional government could not be safely entrusted to colonists ; while, on the other, it was as strongly urged that the institutions under which Great Britain had herself attained a position of such power and eminence, were capable of being worked by her subjects everywhere ; and that the vast resources of her colonial possessions would be far more usefully developed by giving their people the entire control of their own affairs.

In no part of the colonial empire has the experiment received a fuller or fairer trial than in Canada ; and it cannot but be interesting to review the progress of that country, and to mark how far its inhabitants have worthily exercised the power conceded to them. Because, if it could be shown that evil had flowed from the concession of self-government in Canada, it might well shake the confidence of those who desire to give the people of England themselves a larger share in the government of the empire, as the same objects are equally sought in both countries, and the greater the measure of reform granted in England, the greater identity will be produced with the state of things in Canada, where the government of the country necessarily rests almost wholly upon the popular element.

I propose to give a brief *resumé* of the principal subjects which have, within the last ten years, been before the Legislature of Canada, leaving the statesmen of England to judge how far the blessings of free institutions have been appreciated or abused by their colonial brethren. But before proceeding to do so, it may be well to give some slight sketch of the position of public affairs up to 1849.

It is not necessary to do more than advert to the fact that serious disturbances of the public peace had occurred both in Lower and Upper Canada in 1837-8, and that in 1840 the Union of these two Provinces took place. For some years succeeding the Union, an unsettled state of things continued, marked, however, by gradual concession to the demand for self-government, until 1846, when Lord John Russell, then Secretary for the Colonies, first fully admitted the principle of what is termed responsible government, and required that the affairs of the country should be administered by advisers of the Crown, possessing the confidence of the people, and in harmony with their well-understood wishes. The system thus fairly inaugurated, in 1849, may be said to have received its final and conclusive acceptance, both by the mother-country and the colony, as from that date no attempt has ever been made to interfere with its free and legitimate operation. The political differences and difficulties of Canada have been dealt with by her own people and Legislature, and Great Britain has never been required to take part in any local question whatever, except to give effect, by Imperial legislation, to the express desire of the Provincial Legislature.

In 1846, England may be said to have fairly abandoned the colonial system of trade, as in that year the corn laws were repealed, and the productions of Canada generally placed on the same footing as those of foreign countries. It was not, however, till 1848, that the differential duties imposed by the Imperial Legislature upon importations into Canada were repealed, and the Province permitted to import whence and how she pleased, which was still further promoted by the repeal of the navigation laws in 1849, since which date Canada has enjoyed the privilege of entirely controlling her own trade, and her own customs dues.

I have, therefore, taken the year 1849, as that when, politically, Canada was entirely entrusted with self-government, and also because, at that date, the principles of free trade were fully applied to her.

The protective colonial system of Great Britain having been previously the settled policy of the empire, the province had itself incurred very heavy liabilities upon public works, dependent for success upon its continuance, and many other commercial interests had also grown up under it. The sudden and unexpected change produced very serious disasters ; and in 1849, Canada found herself with an exhausted exchequer, a crippled commerce, and depreciated credit. Apart from these financial difficulties, directly traceable to the altered policy of Great Britain, it must be remarked that the country had scarcely recovered from the shock of the disturbances of 1837-8 ; that the Union had brought face to face the opposing influences of English and French Canada, which time had not yet mitigated ; and that the most serious political questions, both affecting the social and material prosperity of the country, had to be dealt with.

Under such depressing circumstances, the only hope lay in the fact that the people had at last the management of their own affairs ; and with a country abounding in natural resources, a vigorous and self-reliant effort would yet overcome all obstacles, and restore, upon a more healthy basis, that prosperity which had hitherto been sought through favours granted by Great Britain to her colonies, at the expense of her own people. Canada accepted the policy of England as necessary for the welfare of the empire : she ceased all applications for aid to be granted to the detriment of others ; and she has applied herself to the task of developing her institutions and her resources with a vigour, determination and success, that have rarely, if ever, been witnessed in any other country.

In proceeding to review the great progressive steps that Canada has made between 1849 and 1859, I shall, in the first place, advert to those which concern its social and moral government ; afterwards, those which affect its material progress ; and finally, demonstrate the result as viewed through the operation of its trade.

In accordance with the provisions of the Imperial statute, establishing the constitution of the country, the Legislature consisted, under the Governor General, of a Legislative Council, or Upper House, nominated for life by the Crown, and a Lower House, elected by the people. The rapid settlement of the country, especially of the more newly opened districts, soon rendered the original allotment of eighty-four members for the Lower House insufficient, and this evil was reformed in 1853, by an increase of the representatives to 130 members. The franchise has also been reformed and extended, the qualification now being 30 dollars per annum, or £6 sterling, for freehold or tenantry in towns, and 20 dollars, or £4 sterling, in rural districts ; the principal feature in the change being the admission of the tenant vote in the counties and rural districts.

The original election law allowed an almost unlimited time for elections, often producing great violence, and provided no checks upon voting except oaths—while the trial of elections was both tedious and uncertain. This has been wholly reformed by limiting the duration of an election to two days, by providing for a perfect system of registration of votes, and by the enactment of an improved system for the trial of contested elections.

The Legislative Council, or Upper House, has also been reformed by the introduction of the elective principle—the existing nominated members retaining their seats for life. The Province has been divided into forty-eight electoral divisions, each returning one member. Twelve are elected every two years, and they go out of office after eight years' service. The House is not subject to dissolution ; and it is expected that the result will be to establish a body in a great degree secured from the ordinary excitement of politics, and able to take a calm and dispassionate review of the acts of the Lower House, which is elected for four years, and may be dissolved by the Governor General.

The practice of holding the sittings of the Legislature alternately for four years in each section of the Province, commenced in 1849 ; and after a long and protracted struggle, this extremely difficult question, essentially of a sectional character, has been settled by the adherence of Parliament to the decision of the Queen, in the selection as the permanent seat of government of the city of Ottawa, where the public buildings are now in course of erection.

Perhaps the most important step required for the perfect working of constitutional government, is to provide for the complete severance of local legislation from that affecting the people at large. The general Legislature can never properly deal with such subjects, and their introduction tends to distract attention from those measures which are of general interest. Municipal institutions have, therefore, received much attention in Canada, and constant efforts have been made to perfect them, and to give each parish and county the control of its own internal affairs. In Upper Canada a system of municipal local government existed prior to the Union ; but it was in a crude and inefficient form. In Lower Canada the attempt was made to introduce the system by the Special Council, which replaced the ordinary Legislature during the interregnum following the rebellion ; but, with the exception of several of the English counties, the effort proved a complete failure. In 1849, a complete system of municipal organization was established in Upper Canada ; and in 1850, a measure of similar tendency, but differing somewhat in detail, was passed for Lower Canada. In both sections much evil had arisen from the absence of all power to levy local rates for local objects ; and burdens were thus thrown upon the general revenue, which were more properly chargeable on the localities interested.

The system thus inaugurated, was from time to time amended, as circumstances showed the necessity, until finally, in 1858, the whole of the laws relating to municipalities in Upper Canada, were revised and consolidated into one statute. A similar measure has likewise been prepared for Lower Canada, and was distributed throughout the Province during the last Session of the Provincial Parliament, preparatory to its being considered and finally passed in the session now approaching.

The general features of the municipal law of Upper Canada, and which, with some modifications suited to the different state of society in Lower Canada, may be stated as the system in force throughout the Province, are :

The inhabitants of every county, city, town and township, are constituted corporations, their organization proceeding wholly upon the elective principle ; and provision is made for the erection of new municipalities, as the circumstances of the country require, by their separation from those already existing. A complete system is created for regulating the elections, and for defining the duties of the municipalities and of their officers. Their powers may be generally stated to embrace everything of a local nature, including—the opening and maintenance of highways ; the erection of school-houses, and the support of common and grammar schools ; the provision of accommodation for the administration of justice, gaols, &c., and the collection of rates for their support, as well as for the payment of petty jurymen ; granting shop and tavern licenses ; regulating and prohibiting the sale of spirituous liquors ; providing for the support of the poor ; preventing the obstruction of streams ; effecting drainage, both in the cities and country ; inspection of weights and measures ; enforcing the due observance of the Sabbath, and protection of public morals ; establishing and regulating ferries, harbours, markets, &c. ; abating nuisances ; making regulations for, and taking precautions against, fires ; establishing gas and water works ; making police regulations ; levying rates upon all real and personal property, including incomes for all purposes ; and, for certain objects, borrowing money ; together with a great number of minor matters essential for the good government of a community.

The present municipal system of Canada, of which the foregoing is a brief and imperfect sketch, is believed to provide for all possible local legislation, and has been framed upon an observation of the working of these institutions, not only in England, but in the United States, the result being to secure for each local district the most perfect control of its own affairs. Under it the general legislature is freed from the necessity of considering any local question ; and the people themselves have, in all important matters, the opportunity, by a popular vote, of considering and rejecting the action of their own municipal representatives.

Passing from the previous questions, which relate to reforms in the mode of governing the country, both generally and through municipalities, I will now advert to that which has been done in regard to education, which certainly has the most important bearing on the future welfare of the country.

The educational question may be divided into two distinct parts. First. The provision of common schools for the general instruction of the people in the rudiments of learning. And, secondly. The establishment of superior schools, colleges and universities.

As regards common schools, much attention had been given in Upper Canada to this subject at all times ; but it was not until 1846, that it was reduced to a system. The very able Superintendent of Schools in Upper Canada, Dr. Ryerson, is entitled to the greatest credit for the labour and talent which he has devoted to the subject. He was deputed by the Government to visit Europe, for the purpose of examining the best school systems in operation. And after a lengthened examination, the result of his inquiries was finally embodied in several Acts of Parliament, which provide for the establishment of school districts in every part of Canada ; every child is entitled to education ; and for the support of the system, a rate is struck by each municipality, in addition to a contribution of £90,000 from the provincial exchequer. ' Each school district is under the management of local trustees chosen by the people—who are again subject to inspection by officers appointed by the County Councils, periodical returns being made to the Superintendent of Education. The Superintendent himself is assisted by a Council of Instruction, chosen from the leading men of the Province, without regard to religion or politics. The order of tuition and the school-books are settled by the Council and Superintendent. Libraries of useful books, maps, &c., carefully selected, are also supplied at cost price to the different municipalities. For the purpose of providing fit instructors for the common schools, Normal schools have been established in both sections of the Province—both for male and female teachers—and much care is devoted to their effectual training.

Permanent provision is also sought to be made for the support of common schools, through large appropriations of valuable lands.

The system of teaching in Upper Canada is non-sectarian, but provision is made for the establishment of Roman Catholic separate schools. In Lower Canada, owing to the population being principally Roman Catholic, though the system is also non-sectarian, yet the education is mainly in the hands of the clergy, and provision is made for Protestant separate schools, which equally share in all the benefits of the local rates and legislative provision.

The result of this system may be summed up by stating that by the last report of the Superintendent of Education for Upper Canada, there were in 1858, 3,866 schools, 293,683 scholars.

In Lower Canada, considerable repugnance existed to the imposition of the necessary direct taxation to maintain the system; but by very great efforts, this feeling has been entirely overcome ;

and, under the able superintendence of the Hon. P. O. Chauveau, the last report for 1858, shows the following results : 2,800 schools, 130,940 scholars, contrasting with an almost total neglect of common schools but a few years previous.

For the purpose of affording superior education, but little real progress had been made until after the organization of the common school system, when there was established in connection with it a higher class of instruction through the means of grammar schools, which are now very generally to be found throughout Upper Canada, and also, to a more limited extent, in Lower Canada. These schools are also supported by grants of public lands, and by partial contribution from the common school grant, in addition to the local rates.

In both sections of the Province, numerous educational establishments, of the nature of colleges, are established ; most of them in affiliation to some of the universities.

The universities in Upper or Western Canada consist---of the University of Toronto, non-sectarian, which is very largely endowed by the Province, and which is now in a most prosperous and satisfactory condition. The University of Trinity College, which is under the auspices of the Church of England, the University of Queen's College, Kingston, which is in connection with the Church of Scotland, and the University of Victoria College, in connection with the Wesleyan Methodist Church. In Lower Canada, the Roman Catholics have established the University of Laval, which is wholly supported by voluntary contributions, and which, though comparatively recent, promises to be of the greatest value to the country. The University of M'Gill College, originally established through a munificent bequest by the late Hon. J. M'Gill, and almost wholly supported by voluntary contributions, is non-sectarian, and is now in a very flourishing state. The Church of England have also the University of Bishop's College, supported almost solely by that Church, and which, though comparatively new, will, it is believed, speedily attain a position of great usefulness.

It would occupy to much space too enlarge upon the course of instruction at these institutions, but it may be stated that they all contain the usual professors of classics, *belles lettres,* law and medicine.

With the single exception of the M'Gill College, which has long existed, but until very recently in a languishing state, the whole of these institutions may be said to have risen within the last ten years, and they are mainly, if not wholly, supported by voluntary contributions and endowments. It is true that the University of Toronto existed in another form—as a college under the Church of England, for many years, but its usefulness was entirely marred by the constant struggle to free it from its sectarian character, which was only effected in 1845 ; from which date it may be said to have risen into its present highly important position.

The total number of educational institutions in operation in Upper Canada in 1858, was 4,259, attended by 306,386 pupils, and expending 1,512,386 dollars in their support. In Lower Canada, during the same year, the total number of institutions was 2,985, attended by 156,872 pupils, and expending 981,425 dollars in their support.

There have been two questions which, more than any others, have agitated the public mind in Canada, and produced the greatest bitterness and animosity. Each was peculiar to its own section of the Province. In Upper Canada, the Clergy Reserves ; and in Lower Canada, the Feudal or Seignorial Tenure. The former has indeed been regarded by many as the prominent cause of the outbreak in 1837, while the latter has been an incubus of the most fatal character upon the industry and intelligence of Lower Canada.

The Clergy Reserves were an appropriation of one-seventh of the land of Upper Canada, made by the Imperial Legislature for the support of a Protestant clergy. They were claimed, and possessed originally, by the Church of England ; but, simultaneously, the other churches asserted their rights, and a never-ending agitation was kept up on the subject. It raised the question of a connection between Church and State, as well as of an Established Church, both being obnoxious to a large class of the inhabitants of the Province ; and it proved the fruitful cause of evil of every kind. Many unsuccessful attempts had been made, both by the Imperial Legislature and by the Colony, to compromise the question ; but in every case the agitation was renewed with increased bitterness ; and it was not until 1854, that a final settlement could be arrived at. The Legislature, acting under the authority of an Imperial Act, decreed the complete separation of the State from all connection with any Church, and provided that a commutation equivalent to the value of existing stipends should be paid to the incumbents, and, after provision for widows and orphans of clergy, divided the remaining land and funds amongst the municipalities of Upper Canada, according to their respective population. This measure has been fully carried out, and the Province has at length found a solution for an evil that had convulsed it since its earliest settlement.

In Lower Canada the disastrous effect of the Feudal Tenure upon the progress of the people can scarcely be understood now by the people of England ; to the student of history, however, it is familiar, through its effects in Europe, where its extinction in every country has been the result of long-protracted struggles. Civil insurrection, bloodshed and crime have marked the progress of Europe in casting off this burden ; and though stripped of many of its worst features in Canada, yet the system remained, repressive of the industry of the people, degrading them in character, and effectually precluding Lower Canada from sharing in the flow of population and wealth, which was so steadily setting in to every other part of North America. The French Canadians had grown up under this system for years ; but the progress around them had awakened their intelligence, and produced that strong movement in the masses which betokened a steady persistent effort, at all hazards, to free themselves from every trace of serfdom. No more difficult problem could be offered for solution to a Legislature, than the settlement of a question which had its roots in the very fundamental laws of property, and which could not be approached without endangering the destruction of the whole social edifice; and the difficulty was not decreased by the fact that the body which had to deal with it consisted, to the extent of one-half, of representatives from Upper Canada, who might not unnaturally suppose they had no immediate interest in it. This problem has, however, been solved; and by the Acts of 1854, and of last Session, the Feudal Tenure has been completely extinguished in Canada, and lands are now held by freehold tenure equally in both sections of the Province. The rights of property have been respected; no confiscation has taken place, but, with the consent of all interested, the obnoxious tenure has been abolished, on payment of a certain amount by each tenant, and by a contribution of about £650,000 from the Province generally. A social revolution has thus been quietly, and without excitement, effected, at a most trivial cost to the country, which will be repaid a hundredfold by the increased progress of the Lower Province; and yet this very measure is that which, more than any other, has been charged against the Government of Canada, as a lavish and wasteful outlay of public money. One single week of disturbance of the public peace would have cost the Province vastly more than the indemnity given to those whose rights of property were required to be surrendered for the public good. If there be one point in the whole working of constitutional Government which should encourage its friends, it is the fact that the people of Canada have been themselves able to approach and deal with such a question as this without excitement, disturbance, or individual wrong.

The Settlement of the country has at all times been a subject of deep interest in Canada, and has been promoted in every possible way. Emigrants are received on arrival at the quarantine harbour, where hospitals and medical care are provided free of charge ; they receive from Government officers reliable information on every point necessary for their welfare. In case of destitution, they are forwarded to their friends ; and every effort is made to protect them from the frauds and impositions of designing persons, to which they are so much exposed at New York.

Leading roads are opened by the Government in the remoter parts of the Province, and free grants of land are made upon them—the price of ordinary land in these townships is fixed at 70 cents, or about 3s. sterling, per acre, for cash, or 4s. sterling (1 dollar), if on credit. To enable large proprietors or small communities to establish united settlements, townships of 50,000 acres are offered for sale at 2s. sterling, per acre, for cash, subject to conditions of settlement. By these arrangements, it is within the power of almost every one to become the proprietor of a farm, with a free title for ever, and subject to no other charges than the settlers themselves, under the municipal system, choose to impose ; while the education law provides for the gradual establishment and maintenance of schools.

The action of the Government in the settlement of a new district, is confined to the opening of the leading county road, as it may be termed. No further expenditure is made from the public chest, as the municipal system makes ample provision for all the further local wants of the people. Under this plan an expenditure of public money to the extent of about £15,000 per annum takes place, and it has produced the construction of hundreds of miles of road in the interior of the country, rendering accessible millions of acres of fine land, which through its sale gradually reimburses the public exchequer.

For the construction and maintenance of macadamized, plank and gravel roads, the Legislature has provided, through a general law, for the organization of road companies. This law has been very generally acted upon in Upper or Western Canada, and instead of almost impassable tracks through the forest, the country is now traversed by excellent roads through all its more settled parts.

The very valuable Fisheries of the Gulf and River St. Lawrence, as well as of the Great Lakes, have also formed the subject of legislative care ; and in 1858, an Act was passed providing for their protection and proper management. This Act has as yet been too short a time in operation to permit reference to results achieved ; but there can be no doubt that it will be fraught with the greatest public advantage, especially in the River St. Lawrence, where the fisheries are perfectly inexhaustible, under proper supervision, and where, from the severity of the climate, the inhabitants are mainly dependent upon them. A hardy class of seamen will hereby be provided, and a new source of wealth and trade be developed.

In attending to the great interests of the people, the Legislature have not neglected those subjects which now so largely interest philanthropic minds. The care of lunatics has engrossed much attention, and admirable asylums are provided for them, where they receive the most skilful and approved treatment. In Upper Canada, a local rate provides for a large part of the expenditure ; but legislative aid is required to the extent of about £12,500, with an equal sum for similar institutions in Lower Canada.

As regards criminals, a Provincial Penitentiary receives those to whom a long period of servitude is attached ; they are there taught various trades, and compelled to contribute to the cost of their own maintenance. Their labour is let out by contract to tradesmen, and by employment, and the acquisition of the knowledge of some handicraft, the endeavour is made to provide them, on their return to society, with the means of gaining an honest livelihood, without the temptation of want to cause their recurrence to evil courses. For the reformation of the young, reformatory prisons, have been opened within the last year, under an Act passed in 1858 ; and by careful and judicious training it is hoped that many juvenile offenders may be reclaimed. As regards the prisons generally, by the Act of 1858, a Government inspection, of the most searching kind, has been established, and it is hoped will be effectual in remedying much of the evil and misery of the indiscriminate confinement of criminals.

Nor has science been wholly overlooked—Canada having had, since 1844, under the able superintendence of Sir William Logan, F. R. S., a systematic geological survey in progress, which has already been of the greatest value to the Province, whilst it has made no mean contributions to the stock of knowledge in this very interesting science. The annual reports of the geological survey of Canada, may be appealed to as evidence of the value and extent of the service performed ; while the display of speci-mens at the London and Paris exhibitions, amply demonstrated its practical character.

The Toronto Observatory is also well known for its valuable contributions to astronomical and meteorological science ; and that at Quebec is also rising into deserved notice. My space will not, however, permit me to do more than notice the fact that such institutions exist, and are valued and promoted in Canada, afford-ing evidence that the progress of the country is not confined wholly to material objects.

Among other reforms which have characterized the legislation of Canada, during the past ten years, the criminal law has been carefully revised and amended ; while in Upper Canada, where English law prevails, the proceedings of the courts have been greatly simplified, and stripped of technical difficulties ; in this respect, fully keeping pace with the legal reforms of England. In Lower Canada, the whole plan of judicature has been changed and decentralized, so as to bring the redress of legal wrongs within easy reach of every one ; while the expenses attendant on the administration of justice have, within the last two years, been modified and greatly reduced.

The whole statutory law of Canada has been consolidated into three volumes, a work of great labour and corresponding value. For the achievement of this important work, the Province is deeply indebted to the late Sir James Macaulay, ex-Chief Justice of Common Pleas in Upper Canada, who only lived to see his work, and that of his able coadjutors, completed by the issue of the new consolidated statutes within the last two months. To have reduced within such compass the entire statutory law of the country since its conquest, is no mean achievement ; and the removal of contradictions and ambiguities in existing laws, is not the least valuable part of the work.

In Lower Canada, a commission is now sitting, charged by Parliament with the codification of the French law, after the manner of the Code Napoleon. The work is one of much labour, and can scarcely be completed within less than three years. Canada will then possess, in a consolidated and condensed form, her complete body of law, notwithstanding she has had to deal with two entirely distinct and different systems.

In the foregoing observations I have only been able very briefly to allude to the more prominent subjects of legislation since 1849 ; there are many others, of a highly important character, which, did my space permit, I would gladly cite in support of my argument on behalf of the general policy of Canada ; but surely the system cannot be either intrinsically bad, or administered by vicious instruments, which has produced within ten years—

A thorough reform of the Legislature ;

An extension of the franchise, and registraton of votes ;

A complete system of municipal self-goverment ;

A perfect system of elementary and superior education ;

The separation of Church and State ; and

The settlement of the Clergy Reserve question ;

The abolition of the Feudal Tenure ;

Provision for emigration and the settlement of the country ;

The care of lunatics ;

The management of criminals ;

The establishment of reformatory prisons and supervision of gaols ;

The promotion of science ;

The reform of the criminal code ;

The simplification of the civil laws ;

The consolidation of the statute law ; and

The codification of the French law.

I will now proceed to speak of the efforts made by Canada during the same period, in the direction of material progress, and which, I think, equally attest the beneficial working of our system.

Canada occupies a position in North America, extending from the ocean at the Gulf of St. Lawrence to Lake Superior, the westernmost of the great lakes. The River St. Lawrence forming the discharge of these lakes, finds its most southerly point in Lake Erie, lat. 42° ; and from thence proceeds in a general north-easterly direction to its entrance into the Gulf, lat. 50°. It thus drains a vast extent of the interior of the continent, and forms the natural channel to the ocean, not merely for Canada, but also for the States of Western New York, Western Pennsylvania, Ohio, Michigan, Wisconsin, Illinois, Indiana—and, it may be added, for the States lying to the west and north-west of the lakes Michigan and Superior. This great district is that wherein the principal part of the cereal crop of America is produced—bulky in its nature, comparatively low in its value, and requiring, therefore, the cheapest mode of transport to market. The River St. Lawrence, being interrupted above Montreal by formidable rapids, could not, in the early history of the country, be used for transport, except by the tedious and expensive employment of small flat boats. The lakes could only be navigated by vessels perfectly seaworthy, and the laws of the empire themselves interposed insuperable obstacles to the St. Lawrence becoming the route through which foreign trade could reach the seaboard. The importance of the trade of the country round the great lakes was early seen ; and the construction of the Erie Canal by the State of New York speedily demonstrated, through its success, the magnitude of the prize to be contended for.

Canada, divided into two Provinces, still more divided by having two distinct national races, and fettered by the commercial policy and navigation laws of Great Britain, was but ill prepared to develop the superior advantages of the natural channel by the St. Lawrence. But still the effort was commenced ; and the construction of the Welland Canal, between Lakes Erie and Ontario, on a small inexpensive scale, by Upper Canada the Rideau Canal, made by the British Government for military purposes, and the Lachine Canal, built by Lower Canada, proved that, even prior to 1830, public attention was directed to the importance of securing a share of the trade of the great lakes.

The wonderful rapidity with which the States bordering on the lake-waters filled up—the rush of emigration from all parts towards them—the growth of cities and the extension of commerce, increased the efforts to facilitate communication between this district and the ocean. But the unfortunate insurrection in Canada of 1837–38, paralysed all her efforts, and years elapsed before they could be renewed. The first step was taken under Lord Sydenham, in 1841, after the union of Upper with Lower Canada, when the Imperial Government granted their guarantee for a loan of £1,500,000, to promote the enlargement of the Welland Canal, and the construction of canals to obviate the rapids of the St. Lawrence, between Lake Ontario and Montreal. These works were vigorously pressed forward ; and the Province was still further excited to redoubled effort and increased outlay, by the Imperial Act of 1843, which permitted American wheat, ground in Canada, to be shipped to England as colonial, thus giving an indirect advantage to trade from the United States through Canada.

The canal system of Canada was, in a great measure, completed in 1846, though improved and extended since ; and she then possessed a navigation for vessels of 800 tons from the ocean to Lake Ontario, and of 400 tons to Lakes Erie, Huron and Michigan. But the repeal of the corn laws—an admittedly necessary measure—then supervened, and the Province found itself subject to a debt of 20,000,000 dollars—possessing the most magnificent canals in the world, but without any trade to support them except her own—debarred by the navigation laws from making them useful to foreign vessels—and opposed to the wealthy and powerful influences of New York, and the connections they had meantime formed in the west. In 1849, the legal difficulties in the way of trade were finally removed ; but ere this, a new element had been developed through the construction of railways, which tended to maintain trade in the channels it had already formed, and which could only be met by similar efforts on the part of Canada.

Experience had, however, fully demonstrated that it was not sufficient to prove that produce could be moved from the West to Montreal at one-half the charge to New York ; it required to be landed in Liverpool at less cost, or the whole previous effort must be nugatory. New York was the great commercial emporium of America ; it possessed an enormous commerce ; it was the chosen port for emigration ; and from all these causes, ocean freights to Liverpool were reduced to a minimum. The St. Lawrence, on the other hand, was reported as a most dangerous navigation ; insurance was very high, from the inferior character of the ships, and from the river and gulf not being properly provided with lighthouses ; and the shoals of Lake St. Peter, between Montreal and Quebec, limited the trade to vessels drawing not over 11½ feet, during the summer low water.

Before proceeding to state how far railway communication has been provided for the country, I will briefly state what has been done to remove the difficulties in navigating the River St. Lawrence. Numerous and excellent lighthouses have been built, the system of pilotage has been revised and improved, tug-boats of great power have been furnished to the trade, at very moderate rates, and the depth of water between Quebec and Montreal has been increased by dredging, to permit the passage of vessels drawing 18 feet 6 inches.

The result of these measures has undoubtedly been most beneficial, and is shewn by the rates of insurance now being only in excess of those from New York during the early and late periods of navigation, while the increased capacity of the vessels in the trade has considerably reduced freights.

In addition to the natural obstacles to be overcome, and the competition with the United States which had to be encountered, Canada also found her efforts most seriously weakened through the policy of the Imperial Government, in subsidising the Cunard line of steamers to Boston and New York ; which by reducing freights to, and facilitating intercourse with these American cities, offered indirectly a bounty, to the extent of the subsidy, in their favour, and against the route *vià* the St. Lawrence. The original establishment of this steamship line was unquestionably of great benefit, but the persistent renewal of the contract, when the necessity for it had ceased, and when its injury to Canada had been demonstrated, is a grave cause of complaint, and has forced upon Canada the adoption of measures for the maintenance of direct intercourse with Great Britain, carrying on her own trade through her own waters, and by her own ships.

To remedy the evil effects of the policy of England, Canada has been obliged to subsidise a weekly line of steamships of her own, at an expense of £45,000 per annum, and it is a subject of the highest gratification to know, that the advantages of the St. Lawrence route to Liverpool are at length being thoroughly understood and appreciated. It is now proved that the ocean voyage from the St. Lawrence, upon the average of twenty-six passages in 1859, westward from Liverpool to Quebec, has been only eleven days and five hours ; and from Quebec to Liverpool, ten days and three hours ; these results showing a better average than has ever before been made across the Atlantic, and conclusively establishing the superiority of the Canadian route.

Until the introduction of railways, it was confidently believed that the completion of the canal system of Canada would secure to her a large share of the western trade ; but not only did railways tend to retain the trade in existing channels, but their immediate effect was to divert from the St. Lawrence a large proportion of the trade of Western Canada itself. It became evident that the facilities thus afforded for rapid and uninterrupted intercourse with the Atlantic cities, would more than counterbalance the greater cheapness of the St. Lawrence during the season of navigation, and that unless Canada could combine with her unrivalled inland navigation, a railroad system connected therewith, and mutually sustaining each other, the whole of her large outlay must for ever remain unproductive.

In undertaking the construction of a railway system passing through Canada, which should connect the great lakes with the ocean, the Province did not propose to effect this entirely through its own resources ; the Legislature only sought to offer such inducements to capitalists as might cause their attention to be directed to Canada, believing that such works as railways, the success of which is almost wholly dependent upon attention to details, were better under private management than under that of the Government.

In 1849, an Act was passed pledging a 6 per cent. guarantee by the Province on one-half the cost of all railways of 75 miles miles in extent. And under this Act, the Great Western, the Northern, and the St. Lawrence and Atlantic, (now part of the Grand Trunk) were commenced. Subsequently, in 1852, fearing the effect of an indiscriminate guarantee, this law was repealed, and the guarantee of one-half the cost confined to one Main Trunk Line of Railway throughout the Province. In 1852, the Grand Trunk Line from Montreal to Toronto, and from Quebec to Rivière-du-Loup, was incorporated as part of the Main Trunk Line, with a stipulated advance by way of loan of £3,000 per mile, the line from Quebec to Richmond having already been commenced as part of the Main Trunk Line under the original Act. In 1853, Acts were passed providing for the amalgamation of all the companies forming the Main Trunk Line, with powers to construct the Victoria Bridge, connecting the lines west of Montreal with those leading to Quebec and Portland, and also authorizing the lease, in perpetuity, of the American line, connecting the Canadian railway system with the ocean at Portland, U. S., which, from its admirable harbour, and from being the nearest port to the St. Lawrence, was selected as the point through which the winter trade of Canada could be most advantageously carried on. This city is, therefore, now the Atlantic terminus of the Canadian railway system in winter, and has been adopted as the port to which the Canadian line of steamships ply while the navigation of the St. Lawrence is interrupted. Efforts have been repeatedly made, as well by Canada as by New Brunswick and Nova Scotia, to induce the Imperial Government to promote the extension of the Grand Trunk Railway to some colonial winter port, but without success ; and it is as yet wholly beyond the power of the Provinces, unaided, to construct a line which is more valuable on national than on commercial grounds.

The result of the legislation to which allusion has been made, has been the formation of the Grand Trunk Railway Company, whose gigantic works are at length on the point of completion ; and of this company it may be truly said, that, comprising 1,112 miles of rail, of which no less than 1,092 miles are strictly a trunk line, constructed in the most permanent manner, and connecting the American railway system west of the great lakes with the ocean, at Portland in winter, and at Montreal, Quebec and Rivière-du-Loup in summer, it presents, probably, the most complete and comprehensive railway system in the world ; and, taken in connection with the unequalled inland navigation of the St. Lawrence, it cannot fail to attract a large share of the vast and increasing traffic of the west, while it affords to the whole Province of Canada the greatest possible facilities for intercommunication.

The difficulties attendant on the prosecution of this immense enterprise, arising from the Russian war, and consequent rise in the value of money, induced the Legislature to prevent the stoppage of works so essential to the prosperity of the Province, to come to the relief of the company, and in 1856 and 1857, Acts were passed giving the private capital of the company priority over the provincial first lien of £3,111,500. By this measure the company were enabled to raise additional funds, and the wisdom of the step is now seen in the full completion of the undertaking.

In addition to the Grand Trunk Railway, the last ten years have witnessed the completion of the following additional lines of railway in Canada :

The Great Western............................	357	miles,
The Northern	95	"
The Buffalo and Lake Huron...................	159	"
And other minor lines of a more local character, amounting in all to...........	370	"
The Grand Trunk............................	1112	"

Thus a total of 2,093 miles have been constructed and put in operation in Canada within the time stated ; while the present charge to the Province connected with those railways which have received public aid, is £4,161,150, or £249,669 per annum, which will, it is hoped be speedily relieved by the success of the system, which is now only fairly connected by the completion of the Victoria Bridge. Reasonable time must be allowed for diverting traffic from other channels ; but the result cannot be doubtful, as Canada now possesses, not merely the most perfect inland navigation in the world, but also, in connection with it, a system of railways certainly unequalled on the American continent, or even, it is believed, in Europe.

Through the Canadian steamship line, the **Grand Trunk** is now recognized, even by the United States Government, as the shortest and best route for their south-western and western mails, than which no better evidence could be offered of the wisdom of the policy so persistently followed by every successive legislature in Canada for many years. The American cities on the great lakes are now opening a direct trade through the Canadian waters with Europe, more than twenty vessels having this year passed through our canals for English ports ; and the time is not distant when the full advantages of the St. Lawrence, as the great route from the interior of the continent to the ocean, will be fully recognized.

In the prosecution of the policy which is now at length approaching its final, and, it is believed, successful issue, the great bulk of the public debt of Canada has been contracted. Enough has been retained out of ordinary revenue to cover what may be termed purely local works, expenditure upon which has long since ceased, and the present indebtedness will be found fully represented by the great public works of which a sketch has now been given.

The direct debt of Canada, including advances to railways, is £9,677,672, and after deducting the sinking fund for the redemption of the Imperial Guaranteed Loan, amounts to £8,884,672, and the payments on account of the public works of the Province, without reckoning interest, have been as follows :

Canals, lighthouses and other works connected with the development of the navigation of the St. Lawrence, represent......................................	£3.962,900
Railway advances...	4,161,150
Roads and bridges, and improvement of rivers....	738,350
	£8,862,400

The public of England can now judge how far the expenditure of Canada has been reckless and unwise ; or, whether it has not been incurred for objects in which the prosperity of the country was wholly bound up, and which fully justified the sacrifices that have been made to attain them.

Before quitting the subject of the present debt of Canada, it is proper I should advert to the outstanding Municipal Loan Fund Bonds, amounting, on 1st December, 1859, to £1,920,160.

These bonds are issued upon the security of a fund constituted by the municipalities, who have become borrowers to this amount. The object was to secure on their united credit loans on better terms than they could obtain as individual borrowers. The Province is in no way guarantee for the fund, but acts as trustee, and has never pledged the general revenue for the payment of either principal or interest. Owing, however, to the commercial crisis in 1857, and the bad harvest of that and the following years, the Province has made large advances to enable the fund to meet the interest due to the bondholders, with whom faith has thus been kept by the several municipalities. But the plan having been thus found to work badly, and to entail unexpected charges upon the general revenue, the Act was repealed last session, so far as related to further loans, and the Government authorized to redeem the outstanding debentures, and to hold them against the indebted municipalities.

Measures are now been taken for the redemption of this debt, which will be the more easily effected, as the Government already hold large amounts of these bonds in trust for the special educational, Indian and other trust funds.

It now only remains for me to state the commercial policy, and the position of the trade and finances of the Province of Canada ; and I am the more desirous of doing so, as great misapprehension prevails in England on these points, and the steps called for by the imperative dictates of honor and good faith are represented as based upon a return to an unsound commercial policy, and fraught with injustice to our fellow-subjects in Great Britain.

Canadian statesmen of all parties have invariably adhered to the faithful and punctual discharge of the obligations of their country ; they have never swerved from the principle, that whatever may be the faults or follies of their Government or Legislature, the public creditor should not suffer ; and supported by the unanimous voice of the country, Parliament has never hesitated to provide by taxation for the necessities of the State.

The commercial crisis of 1857, following the reduction of railway expenditure on the completion of the greater part of the works, and accompanied by a deficient harvest, caused a serious falling off in the revenue of that year ; and this was succeeded, in 1858, by a still greater failure of the crop, and, consequently, even more depressed condition of trade. Attendant upon this state of things, and as if to tax the energies of the people to the utmost, it became necessary, in 1857, to assume the payment of interest on the railway advances, with the exception of the Great Western of Canada, amounting to about £200,000 per annum, and also to advance the interest upon the municipal debt, amounting to about £100,000 per annum.

Dependence could partly be placed upon a revival of trade to restore the revenue to its former point ; but this would afford no means of meeting the future railway and municipal payments ; and Parliament had to choose between a continued system of borrowing to meet deficiencies, or an increase of taxation to such amount as might, with economy of administration in every branch of the public service, on a revival of trade, restore the equilibrium of income and expenditure. It is true that another course was open ; and that was, to exact the terms upon which the railway advances were made ; and to leave the holders of the municipal bonds to collect their interest, under the strict letter of the law. By these steps Canada would certainly have relieved herself from the pressure of increased taxation, and might have escaped the reproaches of those who blame the increase of her customs duties. But it would have been at the expense of the English capitalists who had placed their faith in the fair treatment of her Government and Legislature ; and it would have been but poor consolation for them to know, that, through their loss, Canada was able to admit British goods at 15 instead of 20 per cent.

The writer has been reproached in this country as the author and promoter of a protective policy in Canada. To this he makes no other reply than that the commercial measures which have produced the results he is about to state, have always had his support while a member of the Provincial Parliament ; and coming into office as finance minister of the country in August, 1858, with an exhausted exchequer, in face of a serious failure in the harvest, and with a positive deficiency of no less than £500,000 in the revenue for 1858, he rests the defence of his policy upon the fact, that the present Government of Canada has maintained the credit of the country unimpeached, and has, within less than eighteen months, so far succeeded in reducing the expenditure and increasing the revenue of the Province, that he has now the satisfaction of stating, that it appears certain that the expenditure of the year now closed, will be found to have been nearly, if not quite, within the income.

It is, however, contended that the commercial policy of Canada, so far from being ópposed to that of the mother-country, has been in accord with it, so far as differing circumstances would permit ; and in evidence of this position, a statement is herewith appended, showing the total imports, duty, and free goods imported into Canada since the Union.

The policy of the mother-country was protective and discriminative until 1846, and that of Canada was made, as far as practicable, in harmony. Differential duties in favour of the direct trade with Great Britain existed till 1848, when they were repealed. And in 1854, the principles of free trade were still more fully adopted by Canada in the legislation connected with the reciprocity treaty with the United States. The repeal of the navigation laws took place in 1849. The policy of Canada has thus, at three periods of 1841 to 1848, 1849 to 1854, and 1855 to this date, followed that of Great Britain. Our markets have been thrown open on equal terms to all the world ; our inland waters are navigated by foreign vessels on the same terms as by Canadian ; the necessaries of life entering into the ordinary consumption of the people have all been made free ; our vast timber and ship-building interests have been thus developed, and our fisheries encouraged ; and, as a general principle, all raw materials have also been admitted free.

The analysis of the statement in the appendix gives some remarkable and instructive results. For the eight years from 1841 to 1848, during which the protective policy existed, the total imports of Canada, were £22,638,348 ; the total duty collected, £2,308,499 ; and the total free goods, £509,495. The averages being £2,829,793, £288,545, and £63,687 ; the duty being thus about 10¼ per cent., and the free goods only 2¼ per cent. of the whole imports.

For the next period of six years, to the passing of the reciprocity Acts, and general adoption of more liberal views—1849 to 1854—the total imports, duty, and free goods, were respectively, £29,429,934 10s., £3,937,292 11s., £2,012,368 9s. ; averaging, £4,904,988 10s., £656,215, and £335,395 per annum ; the duty being thus about 13¼ per cent., and the free goods nearly 7 per cent. of the total imports.

For the last period of four years, from 1855 to 1858, the following results are shown : Imports, £30,447,879 ; duty, £3,152,281 ; free goods, £8,868,250. The annual averages having been £7,611,970, £788,070, and £2,217,070 ; the duty being 10¼ per cent., and the free goods 29 per cent. of the imports.

The following comparative result appears :

1841 to 1848, average total imports, £2,829,793			
1849 to 1854	"	"	4,904,988
1855 to 1858	"	"	7,611,970
1841 to 1848, duty, 10¼ per cent	.....Free Goods, 2¼ per cent.		
1849 to 1854, " 13¼ "	...... " 7 "		
1855 to 1858, " 10¼ "	...... " 29 "		

These comparative statements abundantly prove that the policy of Canada, in its Customs duties, has neither been repressive of trade, nor onerous upon the people. It is, however, necessary to draw attention to the fact that, from causes which will be hereafter stated, the results for 1858, would somewhat differ from the above average, my predecessor in office having found it necessary to make a considerable addition to the Customs duties, by an Act which took effect on the 7th of August, 1858, which gave the following results for that particular year, and which must be borne in mind, when it is necessary to explain the nature of the Customs Act of March, 1859.

1858—Imports to 7th August, £3,263,591.
    Duty, £361,350 . . . . Free Goods, £954,845.
    Duty, 11 per cent . . . . Free Goods, 29 per cent.
From 7th August, to 31st December, under Tariff of 1858.—Imports, £2,711,448.
    Duty, £333,454 . . . . Free Goods, £765,760.
    Duty, 12½ per cent . . . . Free Goods, 28½ per cent.

The fiscal policy of Canada has invariably been governed by considerations of the amount of revenue required. It is no doubt true that a large and influential party exists, who advocate a protective policy ; but this policy has not been adopted by either the Government or Legislature, although the necessity of increased taxation for the purposes of revenue has, to a certain extent, compelled action in partial unison with their views, and has caused more attention to be given to the proper adjustment of the duties, so as neither unduly to stimulate nor depress the few branches of manufacture which exist in Canada. The policy of the present Government in readjusting the tariff has been, in the first place, to obtain sufficient revenue for the public wants ; and, secondly, to do so in such a manner as would most fairly distribute the additional burthens upon the different classes of the community ; and it will undoubtedly be a subject of gratification to the Government if they find that the duties absolutely required to meet their engagements should incidentally benefit and encourage the production, in the country, of many of those articles which we

3

for from a revival of trade ; the main object was to re-adjust the duties so as to make them press more equally upon the community, by extending the *ad valorem* principle to all importation, and thereby also encouraging and developing the direct trade between Canada and all foreign countries by sea, and so far benefiting the shipping interests of Great Britain—an object which is partly attained through the duties being taken upon the value in the market where last bought. The levy of specific duties, for several years, had completely diverted the trade of Canada in teas, sugars, &c., to the American markets, and had destroyed a very valuable trade which formerly existed from the St. Lawrence to the lower provinces and West Indies. It was believed that the completion of our canal and railroad systems, together with the improvements in the navigation of the Lower St. Lawrence, justified the belief that the supply of Canadian wants might be once more made by sea, and the benefits of this commerce obtained for our own merchants and forwarders. Under this conviction, it was determined by the Government to apply the principle of *ad valorem* duties (which already extended to all manufactured goods), to the remaining articles in our tariff. The principal articles on which it was proposed to obtain additional revenue, were cotton goods, to be raised from 15 per cent. to 20 per cent., and iron, steel, &c., from 5 per cent. to 10 per cent. This was the whole extent of increased taxation, and it was expected to yield £100,000 additional. The changes in teas, sugars, &c., were all merely nominal, and as already explained, were proposed as being upon a more correct principle. The imports for the first three quarters of 1859, say to 30th September—have been—

Imports, £5,403,393 ; duty, £730,640 ; free goods, £1,594,468 ; the duty being 13½ on the imports, and the free goods being 29 per cent. of the whole.

By this statement, it is shown that the increased rate of duty as compared with the tariff of 1858, as given previously, has only been from 12½ to 13½ per cent., which can scarcely be deemed excessive ; while so far from the apprehensions entertained of a diminution of imports and consequent loss of revenue being verified, in both cases the estimates of the Government are borne out as nearly as could be expected, considering the state of the country and its gradual recovery from depression. Until the close of the year, the comparison cannot fairly be made, inasmuch as we are only now beginning to benefit from our late good harvest ; but as an indication of the result, it may be stated, that in the case of cotton goods, which were raised from 15 to 20 per cent., the importations for the first nine months of 1857-8 and 9, were as follows :

$$1857 \dots \dots \pounds89,993$$
$$1858 \dots \dots 58,823$$
$$1859 \dots \dots 88,844$$

I can also point with satisfaction to the fact, that the proportion which free goods bear to the whole importation, is exactly that of 1858, and of the average for the four previous years, viz : 29 per cent. of the imports ; indicating that the new tariff has not produced any disturbance of trade, nor checked importations : for it is remarkable that where so large an increase has taken place in the imports, as from £4,520,993, in the first nine months of 1858, to £5,403,393 5s., in the corresponding period of 1859, the proportion of free goods to the whole remains the same.

I will now proceed to indicate the causes which have induced the Government and Legislature of Canada to seek, in an increase of their Customs duties, the means of meeting the large and unexpected demands upon them. But before finally leaving the subject of the burdens upon the people of Canada, it is proper to remark that the rate of duty levied under the present tariff of 1859, covering the cost of all our canal and railway expenditure, is only 13½ per cent. ; while in the period from 1841 to 1848, when the Province had neither canals nor railways, it was 10¼ per cent. ; and from 1849 to 1854, when it had only canals, but not railways, it was 13¼ per cent. If it were necessary to offer an argument on the subject, it might be very easily shown that any increase of duty which has been placed on English goods, is quite indemnified by the decreased cost at which our canals, railways and steamships enable them now to be delivered throughout the Province, and that if the question were one of competition with Canadian manufacturers, the English exporter is quite as well off as before, while as compared with the American, his position is greatly improved.

In proceeding to offer some observations upon the principle upon which taxation is imposed in Canada, I may remark that the views of those who cavil at the policy of Canada, seem to be based upon the assumption that free trade is both the principle and practice of Great Britain, and should be adopted by Canada, irrespective of its financial necessities.

It certainly appears singular that Canada should be reproached with a departure from sound principles of finance, when, in order to pay her just debts, she imposes higher duties on the articles she herself consumes, when in England itself the same means are resorted to, and no less than £28,000,000 sterling obtained from Customs duties, and £17,000,000 from Excise. If in Great Britain, where such an enormous amount of realized wealth exists, it has only as yet been found possible to raise one-sixth of the revenue by direct taxation, it need require no excuse if Canada has to raise her revenue almost wholly by indirect means.

Free trade, in the abstract, must be taken to mean the free exchange of the products of industry of all countries, or of the inhabitants of the same country, and it is perfectly immaterial whether that industry be applied to the production of a pound of sugar or tobacco, or of a tenpenny nail or a bushel of malt ; it is equally an interference with the principle to levy customs duties or excise on any. But it is, and probably will continue to be, impossible to abandon customs duties or excise as a means of revenue ; they afford the means of levying large sums by the taxation of articles of consumption, distributing the burden in almost inappreciable quantities, and in one respect have this advantage, that, if fairly imposed, each individual in the community contributes in a tolerably fair proportion to his means. In Great Britain it may be possible to adjust the taxation, so as to make realized property contribute more than it now does to the wants of the State ; but in a country like Canada no such resource exists, and it would be perfectly hopeless to attempt to raise the required revenue by direct taxation—we neither possess the required machinery to do it, nor are the people satisfied that it is the more correct principle. Customs duties must therefore for a long time to come continue to be the principal source from which our revenue is derived.

Admitting, therefore, the necessity of raising a certain amount for the wants of the State, and that such amount can only be obtained through Customs duties, the Government of Canada, like that of Great Britain, have to consider how that necessary interference with the true principle of political economy, can be effected with least disturbance to trade. And judging of the fiscal policy of the present Government by this rule, it is contended that, with some trifling exceptions, which must arise in all human legislation, the Customs duties are imposed in the manner least calculated to disturb the free exchange of Canadian labour with that of other countries. A large class of articles termed raw materials, are admitted free, amounting to 29 per cent. of the total imports. Another large class consisting of iron, steel, metals and articles entering into the construction of railways, houses, ships and agricultural implements, &c., are admitted at 10 per cent. duty ; leather, and partially manufactured goods, pay 15 per cent. ; manufactured goods, made from raw materials, or articles paying 10 per cent. duty, are admitted at 20 per cent. ; manufactured goods, made from articles paying 15 per cent. duty, are charged 25 per cent., but this is exceptional, and very limited ; while luxuries, comprising wines, tobacco, segars and spices, &c., are charged at rates varying from 30 to 40 per cent., but the bulk are of 30 per cent. Spirits are charged 100 per cent. Tea, sugar and molasses, pay 15 per cent. and 30 per cent.

The distribution of duties on the whole imports therefore stands thus :

	Duties.	Imports.
Free Goods	0	29 per cent.
Goods paying 10 per cent.	4½	6½ "
" " 15 "	7	6½ "
" " 20 "	61	41 "
" " 25 "	1½	1 "
" " over 25 per cent., including Spirits	9¾	4 "
Tea, Sugar and Molasses	6¼	12 "
	100	100

The foregoing statement will show that if the attempt were made to reduce the duty on manufactured goods paying 20 per cent., it would necessitate an advance on the other items, unless such reduction produced a corresponding increase in consumption to make good the deficiency. Assuming then that the duty were reduced from 20 to 10 per cent., it will not be contended that this reduction, though affecting the revenue one-half on these articles, would induce double the consumption ; on the contrary, it is believed that it would not affect the consumption at all, as is borne out by the statistics of previous years, and of the present year. It would then become necessary to meet the deficiency by increased duties elsewhere ; and in selecting the articles, it is in the first place impossible to touch the bulk of the free goods, most of which are free under the reciprocity treaty, and the remainder entitled to continue free according to sound principles of trade. Passing to the next class of 10 per cent. goods, it will not surely be contended that the scale of duty should be raised on *quasi* raw materials to a rate *in excess* of that imposed on manufactures. There is then nothing left but the articles paying over 25 per cent., and it must be observed that they form only 4 per cent. of the imports, and pay 9¾ per cent. of the duties ; if, therefore, it were necessary to make good the deficiency arising from a reduction of duty on manufactures, the proportion of duty to the whole they would have to pay would be increased from 9¾ per cent. to 40 per cent., and the average rate of duty on these articles, instead of 32 per cent., or thereabout, would be increased to nearly 130 per cent. It is scarcely necessary to point out that such an increase would be utterly incompatible with revenue, and that the result would be a financial failure. On tea, sugar, &c., it has been found impossible to maintain higher duties than those now imposed—as they are free in the United States, and unfavourable comparisons are even now instituted by our agricultural population.

Apart from such modifications in detail, as experience may suggest, the Government of Canada believe that in order to raise the revenue imperatively required to preserve the good faith of the Province, and to maintain its institutions, the scale of Customs duties is not excessive, and that it has been adjusted in general accordance with sound principles of political economy. Reductions in the scale of duties can only take place as the increasing population and wealth of Canada swell the importations, and it will be a subject of the highest gratification to the present Government, as well as to the Legislature, when such reduction is possible.

In the foregoing pages I have endeavoured to give to English readers an idea, however imperfect, of the progress of constitutional government in Canada, and its fruits, during the comparatively short period of ten years. I am aware that my remarks only furnish, as it were, an index to the volume ; but if they produce more inquiry and a stricter investigation into the position and circumstances of the Province, they may be the means of removing some misapprehension, and thus prove of service to the many thousands in Great Britain, who anxiously look to the Colonies as their future home.

I have sought to avoid all reference to political parties in Canada. We have our differences, and struggles for power, as in every other free country ; but these discussions, I think, properly belong to ourselves, as from our own people the Government of the day must receive their verdict. Canada stands at the bar

4

of public opinion in England, to be judged, not by the acts of any party, but as a whole ; and no public man, possessing any claim to patriotism, would seek, by parading our sectional difficulties and disputes, to gain position in Canada, through the disparagement of his country and her acts in England. I will venture to add only one remark, and that is called for by an impression which I find to exist as to the political course taken by our French Canadian brethren in Canada. During the entire period from 1849, to the present day, the French Canadian majority from Lower Canada, has been represented fully in the Cabinet ; and with their active concurrence in the initiation and progress of every measure, and supported by their votes in Parliament, all the great reforms I have recited, have been carried.

In conclusion, I venture to express my conviction, that whatever may be the future destinies of Canada, her people will always value as their most precious right, the free and liberal institutions they enjoy, and will cherish the warmest sentiments of regard towards the mother-country, from whom they have received them. The future may change our political relations ; but I feel sure the day will never arrive when Canada will withhold her support, however feeble it may be, from Great Britain, in any contest for the maintenance of her own position, as the foremost champion of civil and religious liberty.

LONDON, 1st January, 1860.

APPENDIX.

STATEMENT of the value of goods imported into Canada, with the amount of duty collected thereon, from the year 1841, to 30th September, 1859, inclusive ; also, the value of free goods imported during the same time.

Year.	Imports.			Duty.			Free Goods.		
	£	s.	d.	£	s.	d.	£	s.	d.
1841.........	2,694,160	14	6	225,834	7	10	146,268	17	8
1842.........	2,588,632	13	2	278,930	7	4	85,944	2	4
1843.........	2,421,306	16	4	241,572	9	0	13,526	18	0
1844........	4,331,050	17	4	441,331	15	2	83,666	10	4
1845.........	4,191,325	16	6	449,960	1	7	59,061	17	4
1846	4,515,821	1	11	422,215	16	8	61,300	10	8
1847.........	3,609,692	14	11	414,633	5	6 }	Estimated 77,139 }	5	4
1848.........	3,191,328	5	10	334,029	8	9	92,978	0	0
	27,543,319	0	6	2,808,507	11	10	619,886	1	8
1849	3,002,891	18	3	444,547	5	1	269,200	7	9
1850	4,245,517	3	6	615,694	13	8	294,133	7	2
1851.........	5,358,697	12	7	737,439	0	2	425,671	5	9
1852.........	5,071,623	3	11	739,263	12	9	311,962	17	4
1853.........	7,995,359	1	1	1,028,676	15	7	443,977	18	1
1854.........	10,132,331	6	9	1,224,751	4	8	703,435	17	1
	35,806,420	6	1	4,790,372	11	11	2,448,381	13	2
1855	9,021,542	7	3	881,445	12	6	2,596,383	13	8
1856	10,896,096	16	2	1,127,220	10	5	2,997,941	14	9
1857.........	9,857,649	11	9	981,262	15	11	3,101,976	1	7
1858.........	7,269,631	15	0	845,347	7	7	2,093,403	10	0
	37,044,920	10	2	3,835,276	6	5	10,789,705	0	0
1859 to 30th September..	6,574,128	5	0	888,946	15	4	1,915,603	0	0

Inspector General's Office,
Customs Department.

Quebec, 22nd October, 1859.

N. B.—In the foregoing pages, the above figures have been reduced to their equivalent in sterling money.

STATEMENT of the value of goods imported into Canada, and the duties collected thereon, for nine months to 30th September, 1859 ; showing the relative percentage which the values and the duties at the different rates of duty bear to the whole importations, and the whole amount of duties.

Rate of Duty.	Values.		Duty.	
	Amount.	Percentage.	Amount.	Percentage.
	Dollars.		Dollars. cents.	
5 and 10 per cent.	1,680,311	6	160,626 80	4
15 per cent	1,722,735	6	258,293 27	7
20 do.	10,784,512	41	2,157,205 76	60
25 do.	216,917		54,049 25	1
Tea, Sugar and Molasses...... { Specific and }	3,142,974	11	579,921 04	16
Other Articles............... { over 25 per cent. }	1,087,372	4	345,707 60	9
Free Goods....................	7,662,412	29		
Total......................	26,296,513	100	3,555,803 72	100

Inspector General's Office,
Customs Department.

Quebec, 22nd October, 1859.

N. B.—The above figures have been reduced to sterling money.